INVENTOR'S NOTEBOOK

A book of fifteen easy-to-make toys with complete directions, all completely new and lots of fun to make and to play with: multicolored glasses, bicycle attachments, puppets, masks, a new game of circular chess, and many more wonderful toy ideas.

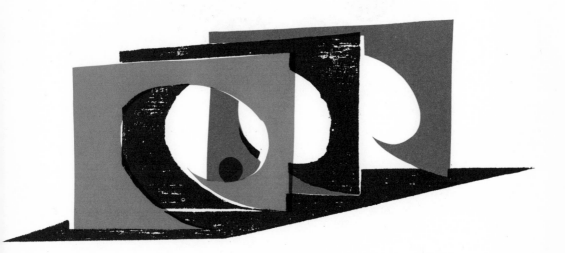

INVENTOR'S NOTEBOOK

Entirely New Do-It-Yourself
Toy Inventions

Robert E. Mueller

WITH WOODCUTS BY THE AUTHOR

THE JOHN DAY COMPANY   NEW YORK

CONTENTS

FROM THE INVENTOR

Here are fifteen toy inventions straight from my notebook. Every one is entirely new. You cannot buy them in a toy store because no one has thought of them before. But you can make them quite easily from my directions.

I thought that seeing me at work inventing toys might give you an idea how an inventor invents. Perhaps you will have an idea or two yourself (or an improvement on my ideas) after you have made some of these toys. I hope so.

I am including an early patent of mine to show you how the United States Patent Office protects an invention.

Have fun with the inventions!

BOB MUELLER, THE INVENTOR

1 | Multicolored Glasses

I used to like to look at the world through rose-colored cellophane. One day I thought things would be more colorful if I put differently colored cellophane on a pair of glasses. Then I figured out how to change the colors and I had invented these multicolored glasses.

MATERIALS:

Red, green, blue and yellow cellophane (or any other colors) (sold as wrapping paper in most stationery stores)

Wax paper

Compass for drawing circles

Heavy cardboard

Newspaper

Stiff transparent acetate (sold at hobby or model-airplane stores)

3/4-inch-diameter toy-car rubber wheel (from an old broken toy car)

Three very small metal washers (from the hardware store)

Straight pins

Cutting knife (or an Exacto knife or a single-edge razor blade, sold in most hobby stores)

Scissors

Pliers

Plastic cement (sold in any supermarket)

CONSTRUCTION:

1. Draw a 4-inch-diameter circle on a piece of newspaper with the compass and cut it out with the scissors.

2. Using the newspaper circle as a pattern, carefully cut out two acetate circles.

3. Fold the newspaper circle into four equal sections.

4. Using the folded circle as a pattern, cut out two sets of red, green, blue and yellow triangular shapes from the colored cellophane.

5. Glue the triangular pieces of cellophane to the acetate circles along the edges, using as little plastic cement as possible. The colors should be arranged in the order red, green, blue, yellow on both wheels. Put them between wax paper and press them in a large book overnight.

6. Cut a 1/8-inch-deep V carefully around the edge of the rubber wheel with the cutting knife.

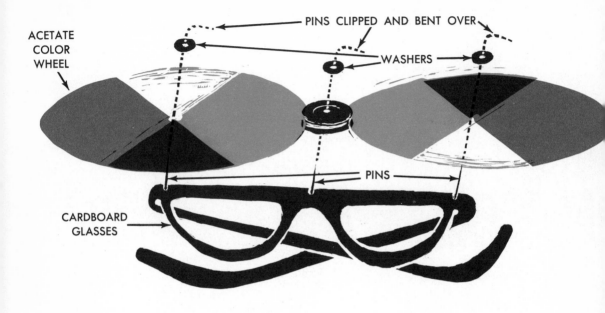

ACETATE COLOR WHEEL

PINS CLIPPED AND BENT OVER

WASHERS

PINS

CARDBOARD GLASSES

7. Use an old pair of glasses or a newspaper pattern that fits you and draw a pair of glasses on the heavy cardboard. Cut the glasses out with the cutting knife, and fold the ear hooks to fit on you.

8. Attach the rubber wheel to the center of the nosepiece of the glasses with a straight pin. Stick the pin through the back of the cardboard, then through the hole in the rubber wheel, and bend the end of the pin over the small washer. (The dotted line in the illustration indicates how the straight pin should be attached and bent over.)

9. Punch a pinhole through the center of each acetate color wheel.

10. Attach the color wheels to the top rim of the glasses as shown in the illustration, again using the straight pins and washers as described above in step 8. One color wheel should be attached so that the order of colors on it is red, green, blue, yellow, and the other so that the

colors are in the opposite order. The color wheels must be attached so that their edges fit into the V groove of the rubber wheel. Turning one of the acetate color wheels should turn the rubber wheel in the middle, and it in turn should turn the other acetate wheel. (The illustration shows the multicolored glasses in what is called an "exploded view." When the various parts are put together along the dotted lines the wheels will of course be attached directly to the glasses with the pins.)

11. Synchronize the color wheels so that the same colors fall over each eye at the same time.

12. Put the glasses on and turn either color wheel and look at friends, at the stars at night, at flowers in the daytime, or at TV!

13. If you are a good mechanic you might try to attach a toy wind-up motor taken out of an old toy so that it turns the color wheels automatically. Mount it in the center of the glasses above your nose.

2 | Periscope Hat

Once I wanted to take a peek at someone behind me without his knowing it, and suddenly I thought up this periscope hat.

MATERIALS:

Two ladies' hand mirrors approximately 2 inches by 3 inches (sold at a drug store or dime store)
Wax paper
Newspaper
Cardboard
Rubber band
Scotch tape or other cellophane tape
String
Straight pins
Scissors
Cutting knife
Needle and heavy thread
Fast-drying, dull-black paint spray (sold at a dime store or hardware store)
Beanie hat that fits well (sold at a dime store)
Colored crepe paper

CONSTRUCTION:

1. Make a box 2 inches by 3 inches by 4 inches out of the cardboard, using the Scotch tape to put it together, with one of the 2-inch-by-3-inch sides missing.

2. Spray the inside of the box with the black paint and let it dry well.

3. Put a pinhole in the exact center of the side opposite the missing side.

4. Cut a piece of wax paper a little larger than the open side, and carefully stretch it tightly over the open side with Scotch tape. (This is now a small, old-fashioned box camera. If you stand in the shade on a sunny day and point the camera you just made at a person standing in the sun, you should see an upside-down picture of the person on the wax-paper screen of the camera.)

5. Attach the box camera on top of the beanie hat. The box camera should rest with the wax-paper screen side of the box over the center button of the beanie. Secure it by Scotch-taping it to a cardboard wedge sewn to the beanie as shown in the illustration. (This illustration is also an exploded view showing how the various sections of the periscope hat go together.)

6. Make a long, three-sided box out of cardboard, 3 inches wide and about 4 inches deep. This box should be long enough to fit from the top of the box camera down to your eyes, as shown in the illustration. Spray the inside of the long box black and let it dry. Attach this box to the top of the box camera (as shown in the illustration), with two straight pins at the pivot points. The illustration shows the front before it is attached, the dotted lines indicating where it should fit. The pivot points on each side are where the straight pins are stuck through to secure the two sections together. Put a small square of Scotch tape over each pinhead to keep it in place.

7. Shape the long box with scissors so that it fits snugly over your face and eyes on the sides when it is pulled down (with the beanie on your head, as shown in the illustration).

8. Attach one of the hand mirrors to the top of the long box with Scotch tape, and attach the other mirror to the bottom facing your eyes, the mirrored sides both facing out. You will have to attach the mirrors loosely so that you can adjust them until you can see the picture on the wax-paper screen when you look into the bottom mirror with the beanie mounted on your head. (If the picture is too dim, punch the pinhole made in step 3 slightly larger in the box camera.) Vary the angles of the mirrors until they are correct and secure them both tightly with Scotch tape. Cut the edges of the long cardboard box behind the bottom mirror, bend the sides of the cardboard down to the back of the mirror, and Scotch-tape it there to reinforce the mounting at the correct angle. Leave the top mirror so that you can adjust it by re-Scotch-taping it.

9. Attach a rubber band with straight pins across the top of the contraption to keep it retracted up off your eyes. Attach a loop of string at the bottom near the bottom mirror so that you can pull it down over your eyes to take a look when you want.

10. Decorate it all with crepe paper like a fancy hat if you want. Have fun peeking behind you!

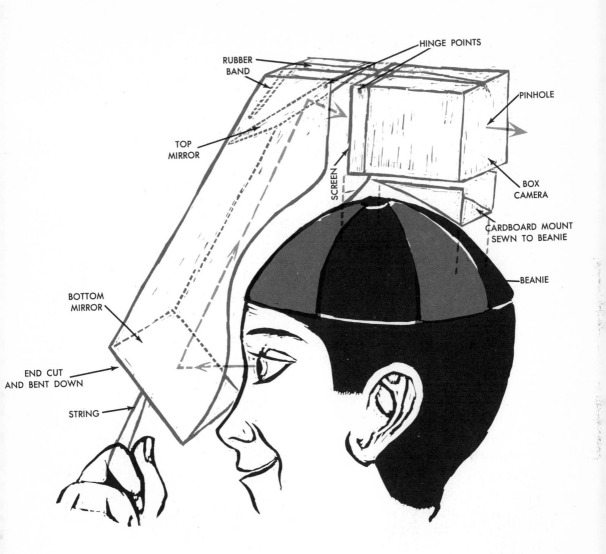

HINGE POINTS

RUBBER
BAND

PINHOLE

TOP
MIRROR

SCREEN

BOX
CAMERA

CARDBOARD MOUNT
SEWN TO BEANIE

BEANIE

BOTTOM
MIRROR

END CUT
AND BENT DOWN

STRING

3 | Distance-Measuring Flashlight

A rangefinder in a camera measures distances by measuring angles. One day it gave me this idea. I thought of splitting a flashlight beam into two colored beams by mirrors. Adjusting a mirror to bring the beams together on a distant object would measure the angles between the beams and therefore the distance to the object. One or two check points determined the distances and I had invented a rangefinder distance-measuring flashlight. This is complicated to make but it is a lot of fun to use.

MATERIALS:

Cardboard
Two ladies' hand mirrors
   2 inches by 3 inches
Red and blue cellophane
Straight pins
Rubber bands
Plastic cement

Burnt wooden matches
Chalk
Scotch tape
Cutting knife
Sharp-focus flashlight
Yardstick

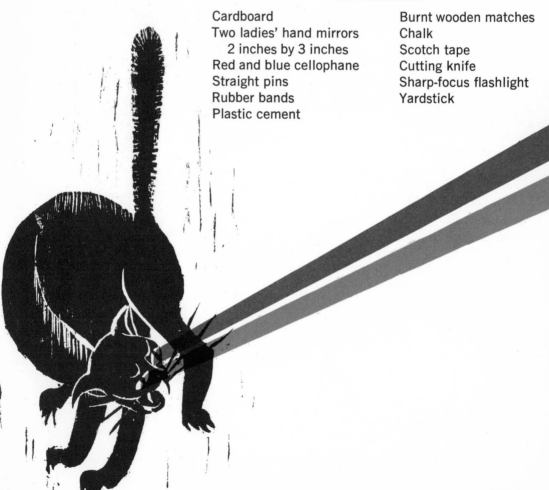

CONSTRUCTION:

1. From the cardboard make a box 2 1/4 inches wide by 2 inches deep by 10 inches long, and leave the top lid folded open.

2. Cut two half-inch round holes in one side of this box near one end and about 1/16 inch apart as shown in the illustration.

3. Cut two 1 1/2-inch squares out of the side opposite the round holes, each 1/2 inch from the ends.

4. Scotch-tape red cellophane on the inside of one of the two square holes and blue cellophane into the other.

5. Scotch-tape one of the hand mirrors (1) permanently so that the flashlight shining through the two round holes will be split in two, one beam going straight out one square hole and through one colored cellophane window, and the other being reflected by the mirror down the length of the box (as indicated by the small arrows in the illustration).

6. Scotch-tape the flashlight very securely with its lens over the two small holes.

7. Loop a small rubber band around the other mirror (2) and Scotch-tape it down along the edge of the mirrored side. Attach Scotch tape hinges to the other edge of the mirror and mount it inside the box by the hinges, so that the mirrored side faces down the length of the box (as shown in the illustration). With the flashlight turned on, you should be able to make one of the two beams of colored light move back and forth by tilting the hinged mirror (2).

8. Punch a hole in the side behind the hinged mirror. Stretch the rubber band Scotch-taped to the hinged mirror through this hole, pushing it through with a matchstick, and catch the loop of the rubber band on the outside of the box with another matchstick. Break off a small piece of the match and put it through the loop on the outside, Scotch-taping it there tightly.

9. Cut a slice in the long side of the box facing the flashlight, just behind the free edge of the hinged mirror (2). (If you push a knife through the slit you should be able to change the angle of the mirror since you are touching the unhinged edge of the mirror being held in place by the rubber band.)

10. Make a wedge out of cardboard as shown in the insert of the illustration. Fold the wedge after you cut it out as shown along the dotted lines so that it looks like the illustration. Insert the wedge into the slit so that the long edge pushes against the tilted mirror and the small triangular-shaped part sticks outside the box. Stick two straight pins through the wedge on the inside of the box so that it does not come out. With the flashlight turned on, sliding the wedge back and forth should vary the colored beams from parallel, to shining together about 5 feet in front of the entire contraption. Cut the angle of the wedge until this is possible. (Not very much variation is required to bring this about, so the wedge will not have a very steep angle.) Close the top of the box with Scotch tape.

11. Shine the flashlight against a wall in a dark room, and check that you can bring the two colored dots (caused by the split beam) together by moving the wedge one way or the other. Make chalk marks at various distances from the wall using a yardstick on the floor, beginning with 5 feet and increasing in the order 10 feet, 15 feet, 25 feet, 35 feet, 50 feet. Stand at each of these points and adjust the wedge to bring the two colored dots together on the wall. Draw an arrow on the triangular-shaped part of the wedge that projects out,

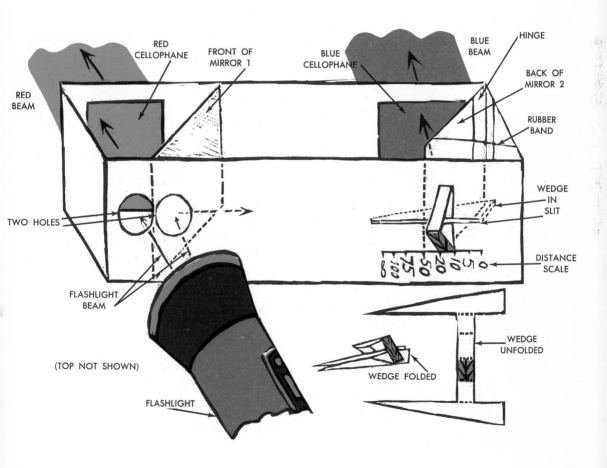

and mark on the side of the box just under this arrow the distances for each position of the wedge, as shown in the illustration. Go outside in the dark and measure off greater distances from a tree or the wall of a garage, going up to several hundred feet. (The accuracy of the range flashlight depends upon how well you make the original measurements and how carefully you mark the distances on the contraption under the wedge arrow.)

12. You can now play games with your friends, trying to guess how far things are from you. Check your guesses with the distance-measuring flashlight. Estimate distances which fall between the numbers. (If you sail a small boat at night this gadget will help you measure distances at sea in the dark.)

4 | Automatic Shadow Puppets

Shadow puppets are more fun than you think. You can give a one-man show with this invention. I thought it up when I had to do it myself once. A dragon and a knight have many possibilities for a play; try to make one up yourself.

MATERIALS:

Shirt cardboard
Heavy cardboard
Tacks
Rubber bands
Plastic cement
Large needle and heavy thread
Wire clothes hanger
Green cellophane
Scotch tape

Heavy black nylon thread
Nail
Pliers
Hammer
Scissors
Cutting knife
Strong floor lamp
White sheet
Frame to support the sheet

CONSTRUCTION:

1. Draw the puppet pieces shown in the illustration on a piece of shirt cardboard about twice the size shown and cut them all out with the scissors.

2. Put the puppets together with the needle and thread, a length of thread knotted and tied at each joint hole. The joints should move very easily.

3. Using the cutting knife, cut out from the heavy cardboard two handgrips with finger and thumb holes as shown in the illustration, and punch the small holes shown with a nail on a block of wood.

4. Straighten out the clothes hanger and cut it in half with the pliers.

5. Put a kink or twist in one end of each clothes-hanger half.

6. Attach the other end of each clothes-hanger half securely to the handgrips with Scotch tape and needle and thread as shown in the illustration.

7. With the needle, attach five threads to each puppet at the numbered points. For the knight attach them to his head-plume and hands and knees. For the dragon attach them to his tail, wing tip, middle joint, head, and the end of his top jaw. Knot the ends of the thread and glue them in place with the plastic cement.

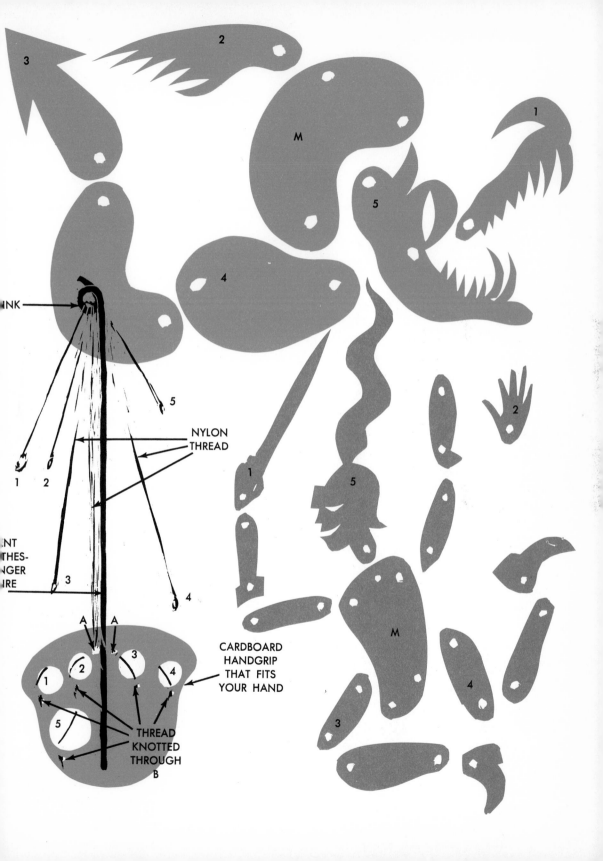

8. Attach the puppets securely to the clothes-hanger wire at section M shown on each puppet with the needle and thread, and cement them there.

9. Feed the threads from the puppets up through the kink in the clothes-hanger wire, and then down through the holes lettered A and to one hole below each finger lettered B. Knot the ends of the threads and glue them down to the handgrip with the plastic cement, with the puppets in the relaxed position.

10. Put your hand in the handgrip and practice pushing the threads with each finger until you know how to control the puppets well.

11. Set up a shadow theater by putting a white sheet over a frame and a bright floor lamp without its shade behind you. You can cut trees out of green cellophane and tack them to the back of the white sheet for a jungle. Make up a story about a dragon and a knight. He could be a friendly dragon and the knight could be a coward. Or the dragon could be very dangerous, but the knight so talkative he bores him tame. Keep the puppets near to the back of the white screen to cast a clear shadow, and when you want them to vanish pull them slowly away toward the light.

12. Now get an audience and have fun.

5 | Sparking Bicycle

This idea will make your bicycle shoot sparks like lightning at night. I got the idea when I was standing close to a train whose brakes began to spark like fire.

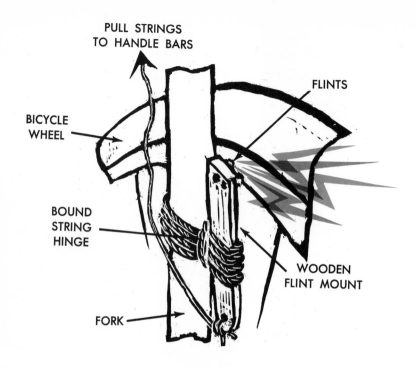

PULL STRINGS
TO HANDLE BARS

FLINTS

BICYCLE
WHEEL

BOUND
STRING
HINGE

WOODEN
FLINT MOUNT

FORK

MATERIALS:

Cigarette lighter flints (sold at all tobacco stores)
Small strip of wood
Saw

Hammer and nail
String
Masking tape
Bicycle

CONSTRUCTION:

1. Cut the strip of wood about 2 inches long and 1 inch wide.

2. Put two nail holes side-by-side in one end of the wood, and one in the other end, being careful not to split it.

Due Sat.

WILLIAMS, ROWENA
ID:31833027681763
V4799 (2 CASSETTES)
The Borrowers [videorecording]
/Norton, Mary. Borrowers.
due:5/27/2000,23:59

ID:31833031675751
V5248
Good Burger [videorecording] /
/Mitchell, Ed.
due:5/27/2000,23:59

ID:31833021692378
V5345
Parenthood [videorecording].
/Williams, Robin, 1952 July 2
due:5/27/2000,23:59

ID:31833031834523
V7015
Patch Adams [videorecording] /
/Williams, Robin, 1952 July 2
due:5/27/2000,23:59

ALLEN COUNTY PUBLIC LIBRARY

TELEPHONE RENEWAL
(219) 421-1240
DURING MAIN LIBRARY BUSINESS
HOURS ONLY. HAVE YOUR LIBRARY
CARD AND MATERIAL READY

ALLEN COUNTY PUBLIC LIBRARY

TELEPHONE RENEWAL
(219) 421-1240
DURING MAIN LIBRARY BUSINESS
HOURS ONLY. HAVE YOUR LIBRARY
CARD AND MATERIAL READY

3. Push two flints into the two holes.

4. Through the single hole tie a piece of string long enough to reach from the fork of the front wheel of your bicycle to the handle bars.

5. Bind string around the strip of wood and to the fork of the front wheel so that the wood can move as if it were hinged and the flints touch the side of the wheel rim. When the string is pulled, the flints should rub on the rim of the wheel and make sparks.

6. Tie the other end of the string to the front handle bars so that you can pull it easily.

7. The first night that comes along get on your bicycle and see how many sparks you can make. The flints are used up very quickly, but they can be replaced quite simply. (The sparks shoot out forward so you need not worry about being burned.)

6 | Zooming Flashlight

This idea came to me when I saw a man in the night trying to signal with a weak flashlight. The long red tube on my zooming flashlight lights up and is easily seen at night. It can be used for fun, or if your dad gets stuck in his car at night, you can lend it to him for signaling.

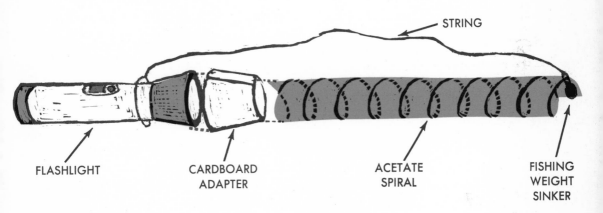

FLASHLIGHT   CARDBOARD ADAPTER   ACETATE SPIRAL   FISHING WEIGHT SINKER   STRING

MATERIALS:

Long strip of acetate
Shirt cardboard
Red ink
Water-color paint brush
String

Smallest fishing sinker weight you
    can buy
Masking tape
Plastic cement
Flashlight

CONSTRUCTION:

1. Cut the long strip of acetate 2 inches wide.

2. Paint the acetate with the red ink and let it dry well.

3. Wind the acetate in a band around a pencil and bind it tightly there with string. Let it sit bound up in the sun a few days until it stays rolled up by itself.

4. Make a cardboard adapter using the shirt cardboard and the masking tape. It should be about 3 inches long. The larger end should fit over the end of the-flashlight, and then it should taper down like a funnel to about 1 1/2 inches. Glue it on the flashlight and tape it tightly.

5. Pull the roll of red-painted acetate out into a tube. Fit one end over the adapter. Glue and tape the acetate roll to the adapter and let it dry well.

6. Tie the string to the small fishing sinker weight. Punch a hole through the side of the acetate roll at the far end and feed the string through the hole. Draw the fishing sinker weight up tight against the acetate and tape it there securely.

7. Open the acetate roll as far as it will go without tangling and tie the free end of the string around the head of the flashlight to keep it from going farther. You use the string to draw the acetate roll back toward the flashlight when not in use, or the weight of the fishing sinker will bring it back if you tilt the flashlight up in the air.

8. The tube should now zoom out when you flip the flashlight, and light up bright red when the light is on. If you have trouble zooming the tube out, untie the string and uncurl and recurl the acetate roll several times until it limbers up. Watch out not to zoom into someone's face!

7 | Projecting Kaleidoscope

I have always thought it would be beautiful to be able to project the patterns of kaleidoscopes onto things. Here is how it can be done quite easily.

MATERIALS:

Small kaleidoscope
Lens from an inexpensive slide viewer (bought at any photographic
supply store)

Cardboard
Masking tape
Flashlight

CONSTRUCTION:

1. Tape the kaleidoscope onto the front of the flashlight.

2. Make a small cardboard tube that will fit snugly over the eyepiece of the kaleidoscope, using the masking tape to join it together.

3. Mount the slide-viewer lens in one end of the cardboard tube with tape, being careful not to cover too much of the lens edge.

4. Slide the lens tube you just made over the end of the kaleidoscope.

5. At night or in a dark room turn on the flashlight and focus the pattern on a wall by moving the snugly fitting lens tube back and forth at the end of the kaleidoscope (move closer to or farther from the wall if necessary).

6. Flip the flashlight, or roll it slowly back and forth in your hand, and watch the patterns change.

7. Try shining the patterns on various objects to see how they look. Your friends look marvelous with kaleidoscopic faces!

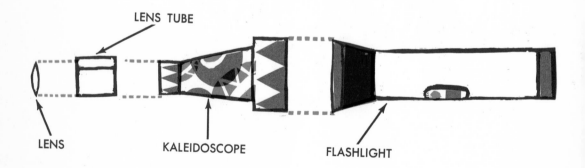

LENS TUBE

LENS   KALEIDOSCOPE   FLASHLIGHT

8 | Circular Chess

People used to beat me at chess, so I decided to invent my own kind of chess. Unfortunately I lost the first game of my own invention! But I still find circular chess fun. (Incidentally, someone patented the identical board a hundred years ago for checkers. Setting up the chess pieces the way I do is entirely new.)

MATERIALS:

Piece of heavy cardboard about 16 inches square

Black ink and a brush or a black crayon (sold in a stationery store)

Chess pieces (sold in a dime store or toy store)

Masking tape

KING'S
BOUNDARY →

CONSTRUCTION:

1. Sketch the board shown in pencil on the cardboard and then fill it in with black ink or a black crayon. Leave about 3 inches in the center and space the rings each 1 1/2 inches apart. Make the double line as shown (along a fold if you want, hinged with masking tape) for the King's Boundary.

2. Set up chess pieces on the board as shown in the illustration.

3. You must know the rules of chess, but if you do not, follow the instructions given with the chess pieces you bought. The rules of circular chess are identical with ordinary chess, except this new rule:

The king cannot cross over the King's Boundary (the double line), except when castling or attacking another piece.

(This rule is necessary to provide a way to corner the king, otherwise he could run around and around forever!) The pieces move in odd ways because of the circular arrangement of the board.

4. This game begins with two fronts, but it winds up with interesting circular attacks around both sides of the board. All of the openings are different from those of ordinary chess. Moving the pawn in front of either knight allows a good opening for a bishop. Circular chess is easier than ordinary chess and the game is somewhat quicker, too.

9 | Gyro Yo-Yo

Since I have always played with gyroscopes and also with yo-yo's, it was quite natural that I thought of combining them. This is a little more difficult invention for you to make — perhaps your father will help you.

MATERIALS:

A lightweight gyroscope which will come apart easily (all toy stores sell them)

A good sleeping yo-yo of a size that will fit into the frame of the gyroscope

A drill bit the size of the gyroscope shaft

An electric drill (preferably a drill press)

Hammer

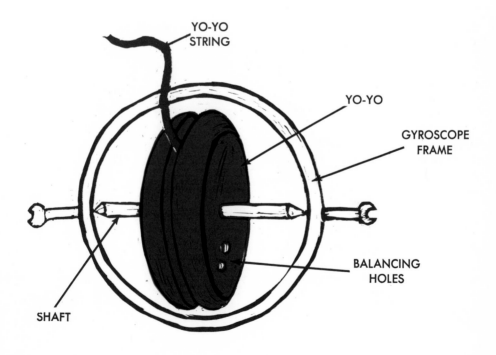

YO-YO STRING

YO-YO

GYROSCOPE FRAME

BALANCING HOLES

SHAFT

CONSTRUCTION:

1. Take the gyroscope apart by unscrewing the end shafts if they unscrew, or slightly bending the outer ring to release the flywheel. Carefully break the lead flywheel off the center shaft with a hammer.

2. Determine the exact center of the yo-yo by having someone spin it asleep, and marking near the center with a sharp pencil while it is spinning. Your pencil will trace a tiny circle, and the center of that is the center of the yo-yo.

3. Drill a hole through the yo-yo at the exact center, being certain that the hole is perfectly true and straight. This hole is best drilled on a drill press so that it is perfectly vertical.

4. Carefully force-fit the shaft of the gyroscope through the hole in the yo-yo far enough so that the yo-yo is in the exact center of the shaft.

5. Spin the yo-yo asleep and see if it is correctly balanced with the yo-yo shaft sticking through its center. If it wobbles, determine which side is too heavy by holding a pencil to it while it is wobbling. Drill holes in the pencil-marked side to lighten that side until the yo-yo is exactly balanced.

6. Reassemble the gyroscope with the yo-yo as the flywheel.

7. Spin it to sleep like a yo-yo, and then when it is asleep, use the yo-yo string to balance it like a gyroscope. You now have two toys in one!

10 | Figured Gyroscope

Little children are fascinated when you attach figures to a gyroscope. When the gyroscope spins and turns the figures dance and spin. Make this for the amusement of your little brother or sister.

MATERIALS:

White cardboard or stiff white paper   Scotch tape
Thin tracing paper   Scissors
Carbon paper   Gyroscope
Colored wax crayons

CONSTRUCTION:

1. Trace the figures shown in the illustration with the thin tracing paper, and then trace them onto the white cardboard with the carbon paper. Make up figures of your own if you can.

2. Cut out the strip and color the figures in with crayons.

3. Attach the two ends together (aa to AA in illustration) with Scotch tape so that the strip fits over your gyroscope.

4. Spin the gyroscope and set the figures over it when it is on the floor. The figures will dance and tumble to the amusement of everyone as the gyroscope spins around. If you balance the gyroscope on a string, the figures look like rope dancers.

11 | Multiple Masks

Have you ever wanted to change your mask in the middle of Halloween? I did once, and so I invented this multiple mask to solve my problem.

MATERIALS:

Two 4-by-6-inch spiral-bound pads
   of art paper
Cardboard
Colored wax crayons
Strong elastic (sold in dime stores)

Kitchen knife
Cutting knife
Paper clips
Plastic cement

CONSTRUCTION:

1. Cement the two pads of art paper to a piece of cardboard 6 by 8 inches, so that they open toward each other as shown in the illustration.

2. Draw the faces shown onto the pages of the art pads, a half face on one, and the other half face on the other. Color each of them in with the crayons.

3. Twist a paper clip to hold the bottom art pad closed, piercing the back shirt cardboard in the middle with the kitchen knife. Or put a paper clip on either side to hold the bottom half up.

4. Attach the elastic through holes punched in the back cardboard with the knife so that the entire mask fits onto your head comfortably.

5. Mark your eyes on the back and carefully cut peepholes through the pad with the cutting knife, two sheets of paper at a time.

6. Put the mask on and look in a mirror to see the effects of different combinations of half faces. Change the mask when you have a change of heart on Halloween night. (To change each half you have to pull the mask away from your face and reclip the paper clips on each side.)

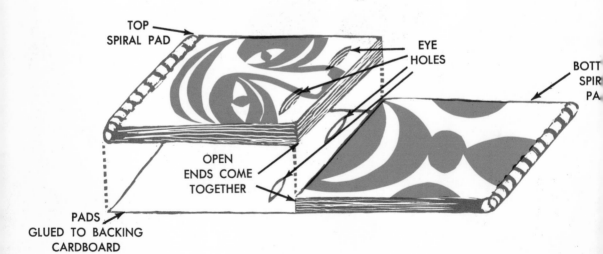

TOP SPIRAL PAD

EYE HOLES

BOTT SPIR PA

OPEN ENDS COME TOGETHER

PADS GLUED TO BACKING CARDBOARD

12 | Yo-Yo Loop-The-Loop

If you like yo-yo's and can make one sleep and walk as I can, you must have often wanted to make it walk somewhere interesting. That is what prompted me to think up this yo-yo loop-the-loop.

MATERIALS:

A large corrugated cardboard box, the four sides of which are the same size, the larger the better (from the grocery store)

Five strips of 1-by-3/4-inch wood, each as long as the shortest side of the box

A piece of plywood as long as the bottom of the box and about 10 inches wide

Cutting knife

Saw

Small nails

Hammer

Wood glue (like Elmer's white glue, sold in most supermarkets)

Masking tape

Rubber cement

Yo-yo

CONSTRUCTION:

1. Cut the corrugated cardboard box apart in order to use the four sides.

2. Draw a large number 9 on one of the four sides (see illustration) with the shortest edge of the box side at the bottom. Make the hole in the center of the 9 as large as you can. Make the bottom curve of the 9 begin very gradually, as shown. (The yo-yo will begin to walk up this curve and it should not be too steep.) Cut out the 9 with the cutting knife, making a slit down the bottom curve of the 9.

3. Trace this number 9 onto the other three sides and cut them all out.

4. Measure the length of the bottom edge of the 9 from the slit of the 9 to the back edge.

5. Take three of the five strips of wood and cut off lengths 3 inches less than the distance measured in step 4.

6. Nail and glue the strips of wood down to the plywood base as shown in the illustration, the lengths measured and cut in steps 4 and 5 in positions EFG, and the section cut off of the strips in positions ABC. The fourth long strip D is glued between them, as shown in the illustration. (The fifth strip left over will be used later.)

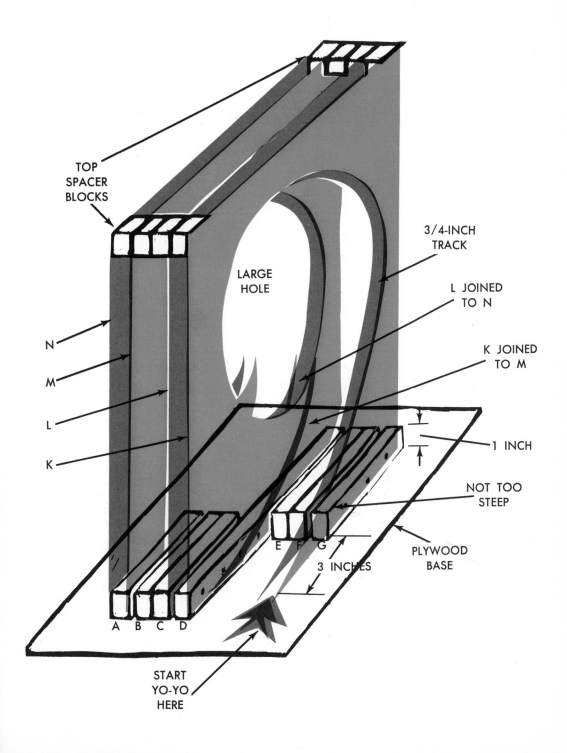

TOP
SPACER
BLOCKS

LARGE
HOLE

3/4-INCH
TRACK

L JOINED
TO N

K JOINED
TO M

N

M

L

K

1 INCH

NOT TOO
STEEP

PLYWOOD
BASE

E F G

3 INCHES

A B C D

START
YO-YO
HERE

7. Strips BC and EF need no space between them. The spaces between the other strips should allow the corrugated cardboard to fit tightly between them. Tack them in place from the top but nail from the opposite side of the plywood to the 3/4-inch side of each strip (with the 1-inch width sticking upward when turned right side up).

8. Take one of the 9's (lettered K in the illustration), and put the bottom back edge of the base against the outward edge of strip G. Nail and glue the front edge of the bottom base of this 9 (K) to the outward edge of strip D, as shown in the illustration.

9. Take another 9 (L) and slip the bottom back edge of the base between strips F and G, and the front edge of the bottom base between strips C and D, and nail and glue them in place.

10. Take another 9 (M) and slip the bottom back edge of the base between the strips D and E in the rear, and the bottom front edge in between strips A and G, and nail and glue them in place. Where the two 9's meet, join them with masking tape and glue.

11. Take the last 9 (N) and nail and glue it into the remaining space, the bottom back edge against the back outward side of strip D, and the front bottom edge against the back outward side of strip A. Join these two 9's together where they meet with masking tape and glue.

12. Cut the remaining strip of wood into eight equal blocks, and nail and glue the blocks into the top corners of the corrugated cardboard as top spacers, as shown in the illustration.

13. You should end up with a track of two edges of cardboard, spaced 3/4 inch apart, going in two continuous loops. Spin your yo-yo to sleep and walk it into the beginning of the loop-the-loop at the front edges of strip G. Let the string hang loosely just before walking the yo-yo into the loop-the-loop. It will climb up and go around the loop-the-loop some distance, depending upon your skill. (It may take some practice, but in time you will be able to get it to spin around the entire loop-the-loop.) Pull the string to bring the yo-yo back after it has gone through the loop-the-loop. You can add more double 9's to lengthen the loop-the-loop spiral and make it more difficult if you want. (If you have trouble with the yo-yo's slipping off the track, put rubber cement over the entire track to increase the traction.)

13 | Barber-Poled Bicycle

I have always liked twisting barber poles and so I thought they would look nice on a bicycle. You can make them all kinds of colors and put as many on as you want.

MATERIALS:

Heavy cardboard
Long round tube of cardboard (from an old roll of aluminum foil or waxed paper)
Wire clothes hanger
Inch-wide colored tape

Masking tape
Pliers
Cutting knife
Nail and hammer
Plastic cement
Bicycle

CONSTRUCTION:

1. Carefully wrap the colored tape around the tube like a barber pole (or paint or crayon it).

2. Cut two circles out of the heavy cardboard with the cutting knife, the one about an inch larger than the tube and the other small enough to fit snugly in one end of the tube.

3. Draw a circle the size of the tube on the large circle of cardboard just cut out.

4. Using the cutting knife, make a cogwheel out of the larger circle of cardboard by cutting large teeth around its edge. Do not cut into the edge any deeper than the circle you just drew.

5. Make holes in the centers of both the small circle and the large circle by placing them one over the other and driving a large nail through their exact centers into an old block of wood. Then take the pieces apart again.

6. Glue the small circle into one end of the tube and glue the large circle with cogs on the other end. Let the glue dry very well.

7. Open up the clothes hanger and straighten it out with the pliers.

8. Insert it through the tube and twist the ends into hooks to fit on your bicycle wherever you want, for example along one shaft of the front fork.

9. Put a kink in the clothes-hanger wire to prevent the tube from sliding up and down. Mount the barber pole where you want it with masking tape, with the cogwheel at the center of the bicycle wheel. The spokes of the bicycle wheel should catch the teeth on the cardboard cogwheel and turn the barber pole as the bicycle wheel spins. Secure it very tightly at both ends.

10. Make two or three and put them on both sides of your bike. Ride the bicycle and show off your new decorations.

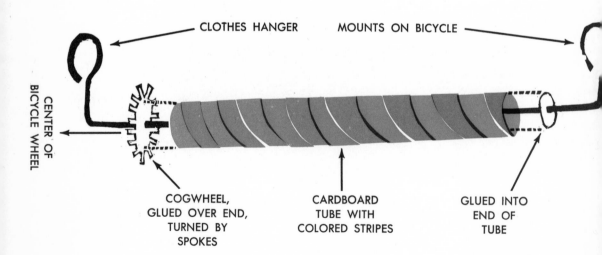

CLOTHES HANGER — MOUNTS ON BICYCLE —

CENTER OF BICYCLE WHEEL

COGWHEEL, GLUED OVER END, TURNED BY SPOKES

CARDBOARD TUBE WITH COLORED STRIPES

GLUED INTO END OF TUBE

14 | Balloon-Nosed Mask

Do not ask me how I thought of this idea, but if you think this is silly, I found out that someone patented one like it with a hole for blowing *bubble-gum* noses! Your little sister or brother would like it; why not make it?

MATERIALS:

Cardboard
Cutting knife
Long balloon, preferably red (and
    extras)

Colored wax crayons
Hat elastic

CONSTRUCTION:

1. Draw a funny mask on the cardboard similar to those in the illustrations and color it in. The tip of the nose must fall over your mouth. Cut the mask out.

2. Cut a 1/4-inch hole with the cutting knife at the nose, and slits at both of your eyes so that you can see.

3. Attach the hat elastic so that the mask fits on your head.

4. Put the neck of a balloon through the nose hole so that it fits into your mouth.

5. Put on the mask next time you need a mask, and blow it up from time to time and watch the reactions of your friends. (The other mask shown uses a thin, long balloon which looks like a tongue.)

PUNCH MASK
WITH A BALLOON
NOSE

HOBO MASK
WITH A BALLOON
TONGUE

15 | Distance-Ringing Bicycle

I was trying to invent a simple speedometer for a bicycle when I thought up this simple distance-measuring device. You can have races with this gadget, or you can measure how many pings it is to school. Each ping is about 50 feet, so when you count 105 pings, you have gone about one mile.

MATERIALS:

Heavy cardboard
Two large rubber bands
Compass to draw circles
Bicycle hand bell
Wire clothes hanger
Masking tape

Cutting knife
Pliers
Plastic cement
Nail and a hammer
Bicycle

CONSTRUCTION:

1. Draw four 6-inch circles on the heavy cardboard with the compass, and two more about 5 7/8 inches, and carefully cut them all out with the cutting knife.

2. Punch a nail hole through each disk at the center, which is where the compass point left a mark.

3. Assemble two pulleys from the six disks, as follows. Slide one of the four larger disks onto a nail and spread cement over one side of the disk. Slide a small disk onto the same nail and press it against the cemented side of the larger disk. Now spread cement over the exposed side of the small disk. Slide another large disk onto the nail against the small disk. You have now formed one pulley. Let it dry well. Make another pulley from the remaining three disks, and let it dry well also.

4. Make two 3-inch pulleys exactly the same way, using four 3-inch circles and two 2 7/8-inch circles of cardboard.

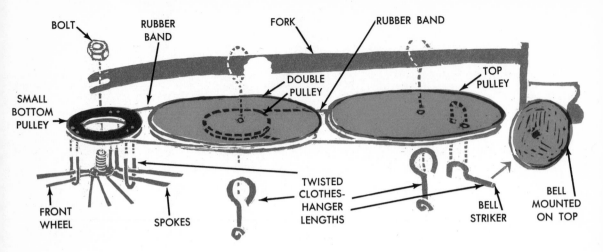

BOLT RUBBER BAND FORK RUBBER BAND TOP PULLEY DOUBLE PULLEY SMALL BOTTOM PULLEY FRONT WHEEL SPOKES TWISTED CLOTHES-HANGER LENGTHS BELL STRIKER BELL MOUNTED ON TOP

5. Glue one of the 3-inch pulleys to the center of one of the 6-inch pulleys so that a nail fits through both.

6. Cut a 1 1/2-inch hole in the center of the other 3-inch pulley with the cutting knife so that it will fit over the hub of the front bicycle wheel. Punch six holes through this pulley with a nail in approximately the places shown in the illustration. Take the front wheel of the bicycle off and mount this pulley in the middle of the wheel over the hub, using short lengths of wire cut off the clothes hanger, bent, and pushed through the six holes in the pulley as shown, and twisted around the spokes. (Use the pliers to cut, bend and twist the wire.) Put a large rubber band in the track of this pulley and remount the bicycle wheel.

7. Mount the 6-inch pulley that has the 3-inch pulley glued to its center onto the fork of the bicycle, using the clothes-hanger wire bent as shown in the illustration, with masking tape to secure the wire tightly to the fork. This pulley should be placed so that it just clears the 3-inch pulley you just mounted over the hub of the front wheel, when it is put back onto the bicycle. It should be mounted so that it turns freely on its wire mounting.

8. Nail two holes through the remaining pulley near its edge and push through the holes a short piece of wire bent to ring the bell, as shown in the illustration.

9. Attach this pulley the same way you attached the previous pulley in step 7 to the fork of the bicycle and just above the other pulley, as shown in the illustration.

10. Attach the bell of a bicycle bell to the top of the front fork so that the tip of the wire attached to the upper pulley in step 9 rings the bell when the pulley turns around in place, as shown in the illustration.

11. Attach the large rubber band from the small pulley on the hub of the wheel to the larger pulley next to it, and another from the next small pulley to the last large pulley, as shown. When the wheel of the bicycle turns it should turn one pulley which then turns the other pulley until the wire tip rings the bicycle bell. (Be sure that everything is extra tight because the vibration of the bicycle can easily loosen it.)

12. Get on the bicycle and try it out. Adjust the bell and the wire tip until the ping is clear. Every time there is a ping the bicycle has gone about 50 feet. (If you want, you can wire up the contacts of a battery bicycle buzzer horn — sold in all bicycle stores — or of a bicycle light, so that when the gears turn enough the buzzer or light sounds or lights, indicating 50 feet of travel.)

United States Patent On Audible Bicycle

I had an English bicycle with hand brakes, and every time I came to a stop it screeched a loud moan. I found that if I pressed the hand brakes hard and soft while I was braking, I could make the bicycle talk like a violin. That is where I got the idea for an Audible Bicycle. Look at the next three pages and see if you can understand the language my lawyers used to describe and protect my invention with this patent.

Have you had any ideas of your own?

Dec. 2, 1952   R. E. MUELLER   2,619,931

AUDIBLE BICYCLE

Filed Oct. 31, 1949   2 SHEETS—SHEET 1

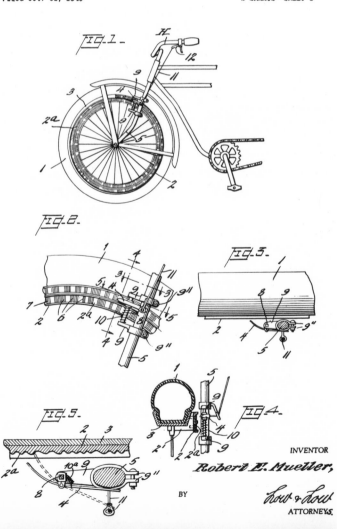

INVENTOR

Robert E. Mueller,

BY

Low & Low

ATTORNEYS

UNITED STATES PATENT OFFICE

2,619,931

AUDIBLE BICYCLE

Robert Emmett Mueller, New York, N. Y.

Application October 31, 1949, Serial No. 124,628

5 Claims. (Cl. 116—56)

1

This invention relates to audible bicycles or other vehicles and has for its object to provide such a vehicle having incorporated therein means whereby the rotating wheel of the machine is used as a sounding board or as a mount for a sounding board, to generate sounds reproducing spoken words or musical notes.

An object of the invention is to utilize a sound track mounted on or near the rim of said wheel to vibrate a stylus mounted on a relatively stationary part of the vehicle as the sound track travels in contact with the point of the stylus, thus generating sound in said wheel which acts as a sounding board to amplify said sounds. The sound track may comprise a narrow annular area on or near the wheel rim, or it may occupy the whole side area of the wheel in which case the sound track itself contributes most toward acting as a sounding board.

Another object of the invention is to employ the movement of the spokes of a rotating vehicle wheel to impart mechanical impulses to sounding reeds mounted on a relatively stationary part of the vehicle, thus producing musical sounds by the vibration of the reeds.

Other objects and features of the invention are set forth in the following description in connection with the accompanying drawings, wherein:

Fig. 1 is a side elevational view of the front part of a bicycle, showing the sound track on the rim of the wheel.

Fig. 2 is a view, on an enlarged scale, of a portion of Fig. 1, showing more in detail the sound track, the stylus and its mounting on the fork of a bicycle.

Fig. 3 is a sectional view, on line 3—3 in Fig. 2, of one branch of the fork, with a top plan view of the stylus, its mounting and a portion of the wheel.

Fig. 4 is a part-sectional view, on line 4—4 in Fig. 2, showing the tire, rim and sound track in section, and the stylus mounted on the fork in elevation.

Fig. 5 is a part-sectional view, on line 5—5 in Fig. 2, showing a section of the fork, rim and sound track, with a top plan view of the stylus and its mounting.

2

The invention is intended as a novelty, yet it may successfully serve as a means for warning other riders, or pedestrians, of the presence of the vehicle on which it is mounted, so as to prevent accidents or congestion on the highway.

Primarily the invention as illustrated and described is intended to be attached to any conventional bicycle, and its operation is under the control of the rider of said bicycle. This improvement or device, however, without departing from the concept of the invention, may be mounted on any wheeled vehicle.

In the examples chosen to illustrate the invention, reference numeral 1 indicates the front wheel of a bicycle with which the device may be associated. A sound track 2a is or may be formed in an annulus 2 mounted on the rim 3 of the wheel by means of small lugs 2', as shown in Fig. 4. This sound track is spiral in form, in its limited extent, and the impressions thereon are designed to engage and cause movements of the point of the stylus 4 away from and toward the plane of the sound track, as it rotates with the wheel. This movement of the stylus, together with the resonance of the wheel rim and spokes, working against the fork 5 on which the stylus is mounted, generates sounds which are audible to those who are in the vicinity of the traveling vehicle.

The sound track shown in Figs. 1 and 2, is preferably integral with the annulus 2, which may be formed from thin sheet steel, with the plane of the annulus parallel to that of the wheel, and with ridges and grooves 6, as shown in Fig. 2, extending transversely of the lineal extent of the sound track, or radially of the wheel. The depth and spacing of the ridges and grooves determine the character, including the pitch and intensity, of the sounds produced.

The sound track 2a is formed in the bottom 7 of a spiral groove formed in the annulus. As shown in Fig. 4, the walls of this groove are sufficiently high to prevent the point of the stylus from becoming displaced by the jar of the wheel. The impressions in the sound track may be made according to any of the methods well known in the recording art. These impressions correspond to what is known as vertical recording, and may

3

be incorporated in a sound track that would reproduce music. This could be done by electronically recording the sound on a paper film tape as hills and valleys. From this tape recording, one could make a die for the sound track by mechanicals means. Such methods are well known in the recording art; and it is also well known that even crude approximations produce surprisingly striking results. For this device it is unnecessary to have high fidelity reproduction.

The stylus 4 is slidingly mounted on a guide pin 8 carried by brackets 9, 9 on the fork of the bicycle, so that when the stylus is depressed into or engaged with the sound track groove, it may be forced laterally by the walls of the groove as the wheel rotates, and thereby be made to follow the entire lineal extent of the spiral groove and sound track. The brackets 9—9 are attached to the fork by yokes 9″, 9″.

As the stylus is thus forced laterally along the guide pin 8, it compresses a coil spring 10 surrounding the pin, and the reaction of the compressed spring restores the stylus to its original elevated position on the guide pin when the end of the stylus is restored to its normal position out of contact with the groove.

The point of the spring-urged stylus is normally held out of contact with the sound track by a coil spring 10a.

A cord, wire, small chain or the like 11 extends from the stylus to a lever 12 on the handle bar H within reach of the rider, so that the pivoted stylus may be drawn into contact with the sound track by the rider against the tension of spring 10a. This cord may be trained around small pulleys or through small holes in the parts of the assembly, or of the bicycle, so that the pull on the stylus will be exerted in the direction to force it into contact with the sound track.

It is obvious that the sounds produced by any of the above means are considerably amplified by the resonance of the wheel 1 or of the disk 13 acting as a sounding board.

The operation of the device is believed to be made clear in the foregoing description. The rider of the bicycle manipulates the hand lever 12 (Fig. 1) to bring the stylus 4 into contact with the sound track 2a, or the keys 24 to bring the reeds 18 into contact with the spokes 17, as the wheel rotates, to produce the desired sounds.

It is not intended that the invention be limited to the particular embodiments shown and described. On the contrary the invention is intended to include all modifications and variations coming within the scope and meanings of the appended claims.

What is claimed is:

1. A bicycle having a sound track mounted on a wheel thereof, a stylus movably mounted on the bicycle frame adjacent said wheel, and means mounted on the bicycle frame and connected to said stylus for engaging the stylus with said sound track to produce sound as the wheel rotates with the travel of the bicycle.

2. In combination, a bicycle wheel, a sound track on the side of the wheel, a stylus pivoted

4

on the fork of the bicycle frame and engageable with the sound track, an operating lever on the handle bar of the bicycle, and an elongated flexible element connecting the stylus to the lever, for bringing the stylus into contact with the sound track to produce a sound as the wheel travels.

3. A vehicle having a spiral sound track on the side surface of a wheel thereof, a pivoted stylus slidably mounted on the frame of the vehicle adjacent said wheel, a lever mounted on the vehicle frame and connected to said stylus for engaging the stylus with said sound track to produce a sound as the wheel rotates with the travel of said vehicle, and spring means on said frame normally urging the stylus and its slidable mounting in a direction radially of said wheel to a locality adjacent one end of said spiral sound track.

4. A warning device for bicycles and the like, comprising a sound track of spiral configuration attached to the side surface of a bicycle wheel, a movable vibratable stylus pivotally and slidably mounted on the frame of the bicycle adjacent said sound track, means mounted on said frame for engaging the point of said stylus with the sound track, spring means normally holding said stylus out of engagement with said track, and other spring means for urging the said slidable mounting of said stylus in a direction radially outwardly of said wheel to a locality adjacent the outer end of said spiral sound track.

5. An audible bicycle comprising a frame including a wheel fork and a handle bar carried on a wheel, a spiral recorded sound track carried on the side of the wheel, a pair of spaced brackets carried on the fork, a guide pin carried by the brackets, a collar surrounding the guide pin and having spaced perforated ears attached to one side thereof, a pivot pin in the perforations of the spaced ears, a stylus pivoted intermediate its ends on the pivot pin, and with one end adjacent the sound track, a coil spring surrounding the guide pin and urging the collar toward one end of said guide pin, an operating lever carried on the handle bar, and an elongated flexible element connecting the operating lever with an end of the stylus, for causing the point of the stylus to engage the sound track to thus reproduce the recorded sound, as the sound track is rotated by the traveling wheel.

ROBERT EMMETT MUELLER.

REFERENCES CITED

The following references are of record in the file of this patent:

UNITED STATES PATENTS

Number	Name	Date
595,334	Paehtz	Dec. 14, 1897
1,031,993	Foster	July 9, 1912
2,367,430	Redlund	Jan. 16, 1945
2,504,042	Ottofy	Apr. 11, 1950

FOREIGN PATENTS

Number	Country	Date
19,670	Great Britain	Dec. 10, 1908

Definitions of Terms

ACETATE — A heavy cardboard-weight substance clear as glass

ADAPTER — Adapts two different things together

ANGLE — Two lines which come together make angles between them

AUDIBLE — Something than can be heard is audible

CELLOPHANE — A thin paperlike substance clear as glass

COLOR WHEEL — A colored wheel through which you can shine light

COMPLICATED — The opposite of simple

CONTRAPTION — A machine or gadget or thingamajig

CORRUGATED — A heavy cardboard formed from two pieces of brown cardboard with a wiggly center

CHESS — A game using carved figures with a king and queen and two battling armies of other figures

COGS — Teeth on a gear

DECORATIVE — Made pretty

DISK — A thin flat circle of something

EXPLODED VIEW — A drawing of something, taken apart in such a way that it is easy to see how it goes together

FIGURED — Decorated with figures like people or animals

FOCUS — To adjust a picture until it is sharp, or a flashlight until it makes a small spot on a wall

FLINT — A stone used to make sparks, for instance in a cigarette lighter

FLYWHEEL — A heavy wheel which keeps something spinning

GADGET — A toy or machine or do-hickey

GEAR — A wheel that is used to turn another wheel

GYRO — A gyroscope

GYROSCOPE — A toy with a spinning flywheel that makes it stand alone like a top

KALEIDOSCOPE — *Kalos* means beautiful and *scope* means viewer: a toy with bits of colored glass and mirrors which turns them into beautiful patterns

KINK — A twist or bend in a wire

LOOP-THE-LOOP — To spin around in a circle or spiral

MULTICOLORED — Many-colored

MULTIPLE — Many times

PARALLEL — Next to each other like the tracks of a train

PERISCOPE — *Peri* means around and *scope* means viewer: to view around, look around

PLASTIC CEMENT — A glue like Duco cement

PULLEY — A wheel with a grooved rim in which a band or belt fits that turns something else

RANGEFINDER — An instrument that measures distances or "ranges"

RETRACTED — Folded up

SCOPE — View

SHADOW PUPPET — A flat puppet whose shadow is projected onto a screen in a play

(Continued on next page)

SPIRAL — Something that twists around and around

SYNCHRONIZE — To get two things working together

TAPERS — Narrows down like a funnel

TRACTION — Good grip, no slipping

TRANSPARENT — Something you can look through like glass

TRIANGLE — Something with three straight sides

TWISTING — Going around and around

YO-YO — An old Mexican toy that spins and "sleeps" at the end of its string

ZOOMING — Shooting out

ABOUT THE AUTHOR

Robert E. Mueller spent a busy youth in St. Louis, Missouri, venturing into magic, art, chemistry and the theater. At thirteen he became an amateur radio operator, and began to invent electronic gadgets. He served in the Navy during World War II as a radar technician, and the Navy sent him to Massachusetts Institute of Technology. During his service he patented a television tube. Later he worked at Philco Radio, where he made numerous electronic invention disclosures, and he is now employed as a science writer. He is also an artist, a musician, and author of a book entitled *Inventivity*.